Discoveri...

Raccoons

by Melvin and Gilda Berger

SCHOLASTIC INC.

New York Toronto London Auckland
Sydney Mexico City New Delhi Hong Kong

ISBN 978-0-545-24434-3

12 11 10 9 8 7 6 5 4 3 2   10 11 12 13 14 15/0

Printed in the U.S.A.   40
First printing, September 2010

Photo Credits:

Cover: © Ron Erwin/photolibrary; Back Cover: © M. Delpho/photolibrary; Title Page: © Daniel J. Cox/Getty Images; Page
3: © Jacob Taposchaner/Getty Images; Page 4: © Frank Siteman/photolibrary; Page 5: © Gay Bumgarner/Getty Images;
Page 6: © Daniel J. Cox/Getty Images; Page 7: © DAJ/Getty Images; Page 8: © James Hager/Getty Images; Page 9: ©
Tier Und Naturfotografie J & C Sohns/Getty Images; Page 10: © Daniel J. Cox/Getty Images; Page 11: © John Wollwerth/
Shutterstock; Page 12: © Bildagentur RM/photolibrary; Page 13: © Joe McDonald/Getty Images; Page 14: © Hans
Reinhard/Photo Researchers, Inc.; Page 15: © Delpho Delpho/photolibrary; Page 16: © rmarnold/Shutterstock

Raccoons live in the forest.

Raccoons are small and furry.

Is the raccoon's tail long?

Their tails have black rings.

Raccoons have black eye patches.

Their snouts are pointed.

Raccoon babies are born in the spring.

How many raccoons do you see?

The family lives in a hollow tree.

Can you see their claws?

Baby raccoons play in the trees.

They learn to climb.

Raccoons dig for worms.

Can you find the fish?

They hunt for frogs and fish.

Is this
raccoon
near water?

Many raccoons eat near water.

A swim is nice!

Ask Yourself

1. Where do raccoons live?
2. What keeps raccoons warm?
3. Can raccoons climb trees?
4. What animals do raccoons eat?
5. Do raccoons like water?

You can find the answers in this book.